# travelling
## to the fish
## orchards

# ROBERT SEATTER

# travelling to the fish orchards

seren

Seren is the book imprint of
Poetry Wales Press Ltd
Nolton Street, Bridgend, Wales
*www.seren-books.com*

ISBN 1-85411-324-0

A CIP record for this title is available from the British Library.

The publisher acknowledges the financial assistance
of the Arts Council of Wales.

Printed by Bell & Bain, Glasgow.

Cover: 'Flowers from the Island' (section) by Neil Drury

# Contents

## The Book of Milan

# The Tightrope Walkers' Wedding

*after the photograph* Le Mariage des Funambules, 1959

They were married on a tightrope – the curve
of her dress in a loop over her arm like a tipped bowl
of sugar, its white grains stopped in motion

at the sight of his arms black and outstretched, light
on the suit's dark serge, long white pole, a glint of wax
on his moustache as if concentration had a texture:

from lip to toe to dark blue eye. He would risk
a half-smile for a moment. She would dare
an encouraging nod. For each other. For the people

watching rapt down below – lion tamer, clowns,
the effete French jugglers, a Russian strong man
with his trail of bent iron bars, dog's small eye.

Even the pool of prickling sawdust, the silence
caught them with a clarity, echoed their breath,
the blood beat in their ears, as all marked the progress

of their soles along the wire, accompanied each step
with a whisper, a hush, an anticipation of falling,
an indecency of hope. Till their two huge shadows finally

kissed on the walls of the billowing tent – a purple arch
all a-tremble, as if touch on touch, second on second
were negotiating the thought of ever being separate again.

# Pumpkins

We are talking about what we will do
in this Hallowe'en city. The last day of October
and everyone mad for it; even the airport staff
wear cat masks, witches' hats, dangling spiders,
smile their efficiency toothlessly, clap each other
on the back at bigger, better costumes. Outside,
San Franciso gleams and preens itself –
knife-edge shadows of fire-escapes on the wall,
cats walking softly on warm, warm air.
I wonder if my skin is some sort of disguise.
You sing under your breath *where has all the fog gone?*
In the streets of the Castro the gay crowds muster:
seven identical 1940s sailor girls, one chucks me
under the chin, calls me *darlin', loverboy, sexy*;
duos of Dorothys replete with Toto in a basket;
a tottering Carmen Miranda who keeps giving away
her fruit, some of it real, some of it not. You bite
into bright red plastic. One white-frocked
Marilyn Monroe stands over a heating grill,
the pleats of her skirt waiting for the moment.
From your room in the Mission – cool, grey,
a painting of a monkey model (armless)
and a blue toy car on the wall – we watch
your friend Louis at the opposite window,
carving his pumpkin, heaping the flesh
in a pale orange mound to one side, cutting out
a smile, gap-toothed, triangular.
It stares back out at us, laughter in its throat.
Later, Louis paints his face in the mirror,
slips on the thin, black skin of a dress.
It glitters and shimmers inside the window, departing
leaves us mirrorless, empty. We keep on talking
about what we will do in this Hallowe'en city,
how to be a part of it, how we'd cut the pumpkin
we might buy, hack the curve of its lips.
Switching the light off, we conjure its taste,
tongue our smiles in the gaps in between.

# Penelope

The toes were not like his, nor the blunt, prodding
fingers. Nor that probing tongue that left her lips
wet. The other had kissed so neatly.

When he strayed from her side, he got lost
in the corridors, called the cook the doctor,
and mistook the postman for a landscape gardener.

Wandering into the kitchen garden he found
the abandoned beehives, hammered the slats back
one by one, then wove white willow switches

into a living rustic seat, twisted and rustled
the leaves above her head – making pergolas, arbours,
new-fangled gazebos. Never spoke of leaving.

She gave herself one, two, three months
to grow bored of him; to decide to denounce him;
to resume her walks along the beach,

peering short-sightedly out at the sea,
listening for the prow of a boat against the sand.
But instead she watched his hands

day by day with fascination. She marvelled increasingly
at their apt dexterity, as he laid strips of putty
on the rotting window frames,

cut and re-hung the warped, wooden shutters
so they ceased to bang at night and dimmed,
as she slept, the sound of the sea.

# Water Tank

It is cool like a church in my parents' bedroom,
and above it is the water tank up in the loft – which must be
God. He speaks in bubbles. He floats like the ball cock.

And sometimes – when someone is using the bathroom –
it's as if there is water all down the wall.
And I think that must be what kindness is like,
as it flows, as it falls, as it comes in a wave.

And sometimes too, I mouth words from hymns,
there in the dark: *Abide with me, Jesu lover of my soul.*
I tell him about the way it is, inside the days,
walking on my shadow. Then I fly through the rooms

in my flailing pyjamas – with barn owl wings,
with x-ray eyes, watching my feathers glide to the ground,
like splashes of paint, like snow – the way it falls...

                    on my father's cufflinks
winking golden on the dressing table, a pile of coins
for the morning bus, the silence of shoes, my sister's guitar –
its long neck straining. Till everything is covered,

and God gurgles in the cistern. He makes a weight of water
to hold the roof down, stops the doors and windows
from unlocking, banging, flying away.

# Last Family Holiday

*How much to tip Myrtle?* my father wonders aloud,
makes notes of expenditure: petrol, food, the farm B & B.
Later he will stride out to swim, like Captain Webb –
to where there are no rocks, no clinging seaweed.
Just sea, the scoop and wash of his crawl,
                              and the years ahead –
a long perspective of undisturbed newspapers.

My mother times the sides of her tan,
constructs a windbreak to protect us from the hordes:
the Garys and Lindas, the *Fuck off Mum, can I have*
*another ice-cream*, unkind Norfolk wind.
All good things come out of her Tupperware.
Soft round tomatoes. Custard creams.
Blobs of Nivea deflecting the x-rays from Mars.

My sister wears a bikini – with no breasts inside;
slips on, off her lilo, in and out of sight.
A plastic doll with too many joints, trying on wardrobes,
highjumping the handball net.
She is frequently thought to be lost or dead:
*Daddy, go and look for her.*

Only day 2, and I have read all my holiday books.
I write in my diary: *Today we had tinned peaches*
*and Ambrosia creamed rice... yesterday's car trip was endless...*
*how easy is drowning, and does it hurt?...*
I lie stiff on the beach, afraid that someone may find
the writing in the caravan. I calm my nerves by calculating
how many custard creams might be left.

# Hipsters

The trying them on was of course
the most embarrassing:
that struggle of zips and shoelaces in a drafty cubicle,
and my mother's too loud, too middle-class voice
asking *Are you ready?*, as she
twitched the curtain.

And the smirk of the assistant, of an age
to be at school with me, as I explained
with a truculence that I knew sounded peevish,
that these were not really hipster enough.
And no, I didn't want the grey flannels
or the lovat green tweeds.

What I wanted, I knew, with total single-mindedness,
was purple hipsters
like Jeremy Slater's in the fifth year,
adding murderously under my breath
a list of other essential needs:
brown button boots,
a black crushed velvet jacket,
sideburns,
a Frank Zappa moustache,
a 150cc moped,
the latest Led Zeppelin album,
a girlfriend with a name like Pen or Jade or Lisa,
a lost virginity,
a divorced parent,
a hollow-eyed drug problem
and a near successful suicide.

But it being Wednesday and a half-day closing,
I was lucky to get
even the purple hipsters.

# Icarus Writes Home

Sometimes he tried postcards
but the writing slipped off behind the picture,
escaped his fingers. And besides he knew
they would never believe the words his,
would pass them back, one to another
like tarnished, foggy splinters of a mirror
they might find at the bottom of their pond –
while they searched for goldfish,
talked in bubbles.

Next he sent packages: feathers
in paper bags, little balls of wax
with the imprint of his shoulder blades.
There were complicated drawings
of his journeys through the air – the colour
the sun made on Wednesdays in June,
parabola of the moon as it rolled
out of view. Or an origami version
of his idea for a parachute, to scale
and annotated – so they'd understand
his thoroughness, know him to be serious.
Still he failed to convince.

His last attempts were merely presence –
he waited in their rooms, stood
at their shoulders, made a lamp in a corner
which gathered darkness on the pattern
of their wallpaper, or touched the dial
of their kitchen radio as they searched for news.
Hovering above them – lightly, oh so lightly –
he watched them sleeping,
their ears to the pillows, heard himself
fall again in the creak of their breathing,
listened to the sound of his dark blue drowning.

# My Father's Wedding Gloves

*Have them* he said, looking foreignly at their long slim fingers,
their secret, dove-grey colour, their feel of age and youth,
when I found them one day under the stairs
where we kept the hoover, old scarves and overcoats.
Fine, leather gloves, soft, neatly sewn – from another time.
*Have them, it's cold in Milan in the winter.*
So back I went at twenty-two to teach my garrulous Italians,
carried them with me, hands from the old world.
I wore them with an Al Capone trilby against the rain,
a long blue trench coat and my student moustache;
observed myself in department store windows
while waiting for buses, stared out the distortions
upon the glass – interrogating my own imaginings.
Which bit of me worked? Which accessory reflected
the whole? The trilby hat shrank its felt in the rain,
then lost its ribbon. The trench coat flapped against my legs,
turned dank and dirty. The gloves were the gloves,
a part of me and not. I tried to imagine his fingers fitting them
or him saying the wedding words or lying gloveless
of everything at night – he who wriggled under a towel
on the beach every summer. But the truth of it was
I could never imagine him. Me with my leaping mind,
my messy emotions, who year after year had watched him
awkward across the tea table as he manoeuvred words
like slow cups and saucers, as he cleared his throat against
the silence – trying to reach me. Alone in Milan
I touched the gloves' grey lines, flexed my fingers
inside them. Then I lost them on a train some years later
and wrote to tell him, saying I was sorry. The letter
I keep writing now his hands do not move and he sits silent
in the sun. I scan the album's wedding photos
for the gloves we both once wore, reach for his fingers
inside their darkness, keep turning the pages.

# Windswept

– their two heads turning, the wind licking up his hair,
blowing a curl straight across her forehead, startled
jubilance in both their eyes. His bank clerk shirt
a sudden white balloon, his tie with a life of its own
following the line of the river. Her fingers catching
playful at his fingers – casual, easy, just below the photo's
thin white edge. And behind them black and white England
glittering suddenly one springtime just after the war,
an elm tree shot with new leaves growing out of
their heads, curve of the valley, mirror flash of water.
Parked nearby, out of view, was surely that old blue
Mayflower waiting to trundle them towards the future:
both hands on the cake slice, *this is the picture*
*of the house we built*, twins in a pram with real spring
suspension, miles of sand castles, nests of tables
and polished parquet floors, the endless ticking
of a Sunday lawnmower, *your mother and I think you ought to....*
But for now the young light catches them, the wind pulls
handfuls of clouds dizzily out of control.
She writes in her copperplate hand on the back
of the photo – *J & me, windswept.*

# The Summer of Doing Things Differently

Hysterical laughter uncorks, after years of silence
in dark glass bottles on the laboratory wall.
The empty classrooms resound to it –
as we play poker for entire afternoons,
write the card scores on the backs of torn up
revision notes (*Wilfred Owen is a poet of pity not war;
discuss. The causes of the Crimean conflict were...*).
We scatter the papers off the top of the art room roof –
flakes of strange snow fluttering onto summer lawns –
long for them to stay defiant there, nervously
wish them blown away down anonymous roads.
Or bored of that, we sunbathe near the swimming pool
(out of bounds since a near successful suicide),
lay our towels out in guerilla encampments,
twitch in spite of ourselves when the gate latch creaks.
We float with empty minds on a faded blue airbed
in the middle of the pool, stare up at sky, aeroplane,
future – a squint, a breath, a lifetime away.
Or we pile into Andy Jackson's clapped-out Mini,
tour the Home Counties pubs – all called *The Cricketers*
or *Hare & Hounds* – and boast of exploits with girls
that never happened (Sue Dashwood, Sue H., Lisa
with the longest legs, Emma who plays cello in the orchestra)
and everyone knows but pretends knowing leers,
flicks a jacket collar up, leans forward, anticipates....
After, after. We pass Marlboros round and talk about
catering college, arts school, university, the job in Nat West bank
that someone has got, a project to hitch around Europe
(someone's brother has a tent), whether Andy will do up
the car with his first pay packet and what shade of spray paint
he'll choose. Faces disappear behind clouds of smoke,
the landlord shouts *Time you lads. Don't you have homes
to go to?!* Out in the darkness the burps and laughter
have a sudden echo, light rain falling across the pub car park.

On the journey back everyone starts singing –
*School's Out* by Alice Cooper, *Alright Now* by Free,
but none of us knows the words to the verses,
fall suddenly silent. The headlight beam of Andy's Mini
seems already fainter against the night.

# Pumpkin Summer

No rain for two weeks
and the pumpkins grow rampant in the July sun:
shiny, orange footballs lolling on the earth.
The garden shrinks.

The Italian lodger sleeping in the spare room
looks dubious at their growing,
walks around the house practising the word –
*pumpkin, pumpkin.*

He forgets it the next day, goes out
to fuck boys in the baked Oxford meadows,
observes the pumpkin progress
with a face like guilt, eyebrows in a line.

He phones home to his papa and fidanzata:
*I love it here: the colleges, the history...*
*yes, I miss you too. But my English*
*is improving – I will stay longer.*

Later in the moonlight, he lies wide awake,
feels every globe swelling:
a sheen of expectation, root like a claw.
The bedroom walls shrink.

He leaves me tearfully – to go back to Milan,
his suitcases full of English Breakfast Tea;
insists on one last visit to look at the monster.
*Pumpkin, pumpkin,* he mouths in silence.

In another week, I cut the stalks,
lay the heavy, orange flesh on the draining board.
The lawn lies reclaimed,
tame as a living room carpet.

# Through the Woods

No dog walkers now, not even
late ones – glowering out of the dark woods:
trees with hot breath, close wet tongue.

No fireworks either, their burn through the fog,
their smell that made all the fir trees
on fire. No actors in the cavern of the quarry

– they came one week when I was a schoolboy,
left rubber limbs, fingers from some orchestrated
film battle, *The Last Valley*, starring Omar Sharif,

and a teacher wrote *memento mori* up on the blackboard,
asked us what the words meant; but we were
blank, in a fog outside, hanging waiting

for something to happen. No cross-country runners
through the treacle of Black Pond where I heaved
my lungs into mud, fell close to water –

a drowning, a calling for the effort to stop
for the first time, for ever; like a recall of some memory
which I wondered where I'd learnt,

the strange comfort of earth and trees never moving
past me, or behind me, or coming forward.
No trees now, just the breath going out, the last echo of air.

# Wild

They were the ones we carried with us:
the cigarette smokers whose breath smelled electric,
their music playing all night
as they jived their silhouettes across the pitched

school roof. The ones who kissed first,
who had another language that was *after virginity*,
whose non-uniform boots clicked dark brown
along the library floor, as they left us reading

hour on hour – the slow turning of pages
filled with someone else's words
then the long returning home.

And who knew what they did in their time after hours,
in the sunburned summers driving getaway bangers
they abandoned in France?

...They were last heard of in Greece,
they were marking time in LA, they had slid away/
gone solo, they were doing serious music.

We carried them with us perhaps for years –
till they were spotted on trains
wearing undistinguished suits, their hair now thinning
under lamplight through trees,

the shape of them shrunk inside the rain.
But they haunt us still – when laughter sounds
from a neighbouring restaurant table
where they are *having so much fun*, are turning

our envious eyes. Or outside in the cinema light
where they revv their cars
and leave us standing.

# Boy Blue

Was it a taste for fashionable narcolepsy
this dropping down breathless in the hay?
Crumpling his bright blue corduroy, forgetful
of his lump of cheese and white square of bread,
water bottle hissing its silver contents

into corn dust. The sheep went wild and random,
nibbling at raggedy hillsides as they struggled over stiles,
splashed down ditches and rootled in waste-paper bins.
Three of them died. In the valley, the village expected his horn
from before mid-day, waited for its blunt-nosed sound

to come pushing through the warm afternoon;
were puzzled instead by silence.
But guessed that he must have gone farther over the hill,
recalled his busy list of tickable achievements:
*Things to do before 20, 30, 40....*

So they listened to the weather forecast,
drank dark brown tea and stroked the cat –
not knowing that morning he had woken perturbed,
had stared at the clock with no recognition in his eyes,
had felt affinity only with the blind bar of soap,

washed away in cold, clear water.
Later in the grass he had watched, near his eyelash,
a silent ant climbing jungles of lines, had heard the earth
turning mysterious under his head, had realised
there were suits of more than one colour.

# The New Life

I sleep for fewer hours. I sleep for more.
Unroll routine like a brand new sleeping bag.
Or crossing Yugoslavia on a rattling train
in the middle of the night
I fail to remember what weekday it is.
I don't know the language, the word for breakfast,
the way they tell time.

I make lists for days: buy a motorbike, upgrade the computer,
give up sugar in tea, empty the loft of shrinking clothes,
the bits of a record player.

In San Francisco I hire a bicycle,
ride the length of Golden Gate Bridge,
watch its lines turn into fog, the city vanish –
wondering what makes an event, an arrival,
and how I will know.

I remember the other lives, beginnings that seemed like
the beginnings of ends: first razor blade, first car,
sexual desire like a new, shiny skin,
the power cut that drowned the house in darkness
then reclaimed each room
as a different place.

Or on top of the diving board, curling my toes
round its rough, textured edge – the gap to reach the shiny blue.
I practised breathing, then holding my breath,
then breathing again.

# Family Affair

Your brothers, sisters, divorced parents and animals,
an aunt in Brazil, a cousin expert on the Italian Mafia –
the fact of it was, I fell in love with you all.
For punk hair, pregnancies, Pater and pubes
discussed with volubility at the breakfast table.
For the talent you all had of discovering indiscretions
like the clonk of a plastic toy from a bumper crisp bag,
of winkling truth out with flamboyancy and thoroughness,
writing it with a silver aerosol across the air.
Later, there would be someone with a dustpan and brush,
there would be kindness on wide trays dispensed
from the kitchen: doorsteps of sandwiches oozing Marmite
and peanut butter, mugs with indecent mottoes all full
of steaming tea. Liked too the fact
that your family car wasn't clean, but autographed with mud,
full of theatre props and wellingtons, that your dog
was called "dog" and the plants in your garden had no label,
no name, that you had bedrooms on the ground floor,
a living room at the top, and your brother kept his python
periodically in the bath – frightening the girlfriends,
the boyfriends who turned up, with never a shortage of milk
for breakfast.That you made me feel I was as easy as you,
as brilliant, as funny, as shot through with laughter,
that the windows in my house were open like yours,
glittering with light and interesting laundry. Not surprising,
I suppose, that you returned the compliment,
that you longed for my family's yards of clean table cloth,
its careful breath of politeness, its rooms of space;
for the dozing Sunday silence broken intermittently
by the bark of a dog called Rover.

# Venice

Some things are hard to believe, some
easier than you think. They just happen,
like daylight, or morning. Like the way
that arms go round and bodies seem to fit,
the little by little advancing of lips till they
stick, till they taste good and the noses
somehow never get in the way. Then you laugh
because it's so easy, so good. The way
you told me that you laughed the first time
you saw Venice, collapsed on the steps
outside the station and laughed right out loud
at all that beauty, at the picture of it all.
Just the way it should be: the gondolas bobbing
down up down, the men in their straw hats,
their teeth – when they smiled – so brilliantly white.

# Paperweight

Now you are inside, with all those bits
of bright Murano glass. One to choose
among galaxy, garden, snow scene over Venice.
Now your eye like a marble, light on a curl
of your hair, the lip you have just licked,
harmony of your fingers and moons of your fingernails
are glass-cased, smooth to my touch.
I can look and look my fill inside – never catch you
blinking. I can never have enough of you.
Now I have you in the palm of my hand,
the warm and the cold of you.
Or here on the desk where you hold my life in place,
stop all my surfaces from sliding loose,
keep the best bits of me from blowing away.

# Wedding

All their clothes are new: the nervous sheen
of his pale grey suit – something in linen,
a shirt starched so white that it glazes

his chin with a strange blue hue,
the unusual flamboyancy
of his flapping silk paisley tie.

She steps from a wardrobe
that he has never seen, where layers of skirts
move independent – with the hiss

of a receding sea, where her eyes
behind gauze float in turquoise shadow.
Kneeling on the step she hears

the squeak of his new shoes, he smells
the foreign sweetness of her lily of the valley;
they watch themselves passing

in the hire car's wing mirror.  Later,
they touch the pressed lines of each other's
clothes, undo them like presents and gasp

with surprise – just like the first time.

# Answerphone

I left you for a space calling out to me
like someone shouting across water
as if you knew for sure I was really there –

holding my breath below the surface,
pressure in my ears, cheeks like a football.
As if I might swim to the other side

with a change of clothes in a knotted plastic bag
and cycle off on a rusty bicycle
I had left behind the pine trees.

Then stand in some bar growing briefly light-headed
on a single glass of beer, walk out into sunshine
with no name, no home.

Oh sometimes I might think of you
as you followed me across the water,
as you spluttered and sank mid-way in the blue.

Knowing you, you might even re-surface
with your survivor's tenacity,
with that tone of your voice saying *Listen to me*.

Then you'd gasp to final silence, a look of surprise,
and leave me just that still, red light –
like a swimmer's warning.

# First Marriage

Looking back, it seemed to happen
underwater.  The shoes were smaller,
the hands quite white, the voices came back
in bubbles like raspberries: I do, I do.

Did I?  Did we somewhere make those lists,
pick a tie to match your bouquet (eau de nil
not jade; we go through every shade of green),
smile for a mantlepiece across swimming rooms,

buy curtain rings and tin openers,
make love in front of a silent tv (our bodies
striped in watery light) and realise at night
that the breathing goes on forever –

each exhalation like a wave?  Water
on our chests in a grey and green column
as far as we could see.  So we swam
to the surface, clambered onto the mantlepiece,

then watched the furniture float slowly away.

# The Goodbye Letter

All day, writing to you, I watch the boys
trying to roller-skate down the street.
The ugly whirr of their wheels burns the asphalt,
they bump off the pavement, then the giddy build up
of their speed, all flailing butterfly arms –
repeating, repeating the glory
of the almost.  Their every success
so loudly signalled by claps, cheers,
fists balling the air, by their noisy determination
that this time they almost did it.
I can follow their progress with my eyes closed,
still wait every time for the successful silence
of wheels gliding smoothly down the street
and away.... But their criss-crossing skids
make lines on my paper, their jeers
are in my head.  They yell and yell
for hours, keep falling, lick their grazes
like mongrel dogs, scrap for praise; could be heroes
for so little.  Then they unstrap their skates
and wobble unfamiliar on ordinary legs
into the dusk, toss a goodbye over their shoulder.
That last bit so strangely easy.

# Making Lemon Curd

I am making lemon curd
while you are travelling back to France.
(One o'clock you take the bus.)

An insanely domestic thing to be doing
in the middle of this black hole of loss;
but the precise imperatives
of the *Sainsbury's Cookbook of Afternoon Teas*
are a sort of comfort.
(Two o'clock you check in at Heathrow.)

Four brown eggs and four yellow lemons,
half a bag of caster sugar and half a pound of butter:
all you need for the perfect lemon curd.
(Three o'clock you fly to Lyon.)

Mix the sugar with the lemons,
and beat with patience for ten minutes or more
till you get a sticky paste that remains on the back
of a wooden spoon.
(Six o'clock your time you land, then
take a train to Montpellier.)

Then beat with more patience,
without letting the water boil
else it mars the smoothness of the curd.
Allow to cool and then place in the fridge.
(Ten o'clock you sleep alone in crisp white sheets,
in a foreign room, your mind still travelling.)

And I have a perfect lemon curd,
stoppered in a jar, labelled and dated
with the day that you left.

# The Lost Glove

Strange how, when your best friend is pregnant,
you walk along the street and it seems
that every second person is....
Suddenly the universe teems with large, swaying women
you must stand up for on buses.

The world colludes with us, sends us messages.
It walks right up to us in the middle of the supermarket,
reflects a new face in habitual shoe shop windows
(*Everything must go*) and turns our head
round the next-but-one street corner –
to stop us in our tracks.

So when you said today you wanted to be freer,
I noticed for the first time how many roof tiles
were dislodged down our road, how one flapping shirt
had tugged itself unpegged
from the loop of our washing line,
how the badly glued BT poster (*It's good to...*) had ripped
from its hoarding, and how one black glove
had been stuck on the spike of an iron railing,
waving damp fingers at passers by.

# Learning Happiness

I tell her the rules of the game
when all the coloured counters are lost –
just an empty box remains.

I tell her it is learnt like everything:
notes on a recorder, tables one to ten,
the days of the week in French.

I tell her it has witnesses: postcard,
post-it, fax. You hold the words in place
with drawing pins on a noticeboard,

or litmus paper on litmus paper,
hang them against the window to dry –
this is the colour it has.

I tell her it is caught unawares,
a zoom lens straight to the heart:
this sudden blue balloon rising

in the seven o'clock orange of the sky,
serene and lovely as silence
above the long grey road.

# Cornflowers

You come upon me in a field.
I am sky looking up to sky
so you wonder where your opposites
have gone. You pitch between sleep
and waking, tell the dream
it is not. But I am what you know,
remember? The colour of every best shirt,
your valiant ink finger, your sunk-
in-the glass memory. I survive.
The sun may burn me out
to wide blue, lost blue, to blue faded through
to white at the edges.
But there is blue in the evening
burning softly in the gloom,
in an ordinary kitchen where I leave no scent.
I stand easy in the jug.
I am there in your hands.
No need to proclaim me – I am no noisy
orange flowers in a hood of cellophane.
I speak your language, leave sap
on your fingers, across your sheet of paper.
Look at my gathering of petals –
how could they be closer?
My sooty black heart –
how could it not say what it feels?

# Living Italian, first published 1955

Giovanni and Mario are always on a train.
*What region is this, Mario? This is Lazio, Giovanni.*
It's a black and white ink drawing with marketry shadows,
where everyone walks with tapering legs, has a penchant
for leaning on bridges, for small dogs or mopeds.
*What a large and modern station, Mario!*
*Yes, it is beautiful and also very practical, Giovanni.*
Living Italian – life inside its pale blue covers
was everything I wanted; so easy, so simple.
*Io sono Roberto* I kept on repeating.
I do not live in Surbiton. I live in Milano, Roma, Venezia.
'*Bello, bello* – sometimes to make the superlative,
you simply repeat the adjective in Italian.'
Life as simple as this. Joy as simple, simple as this.
*This church was built by Brunelleschi, Giovanni.*
*Oh thank you, thank you, Mario!*
This was what I wanted. Morning was Botticelli, Leonardo.
Afternoon was following Mario's long legs
along the Ponte Vecchio. *Let us stop for a picnic.*
*Oh yes, do let us! What's in your picnic basket, Mario?*
*I have two pieces of ham, some fine Dolcelatte cheese,*
*two rolls, a small flask of wine, a packet of salt*
*and even a paper napkin.* Not spaghetti loops out of a tin,
not Kraft cheese sandwich squares wrapped in plastic,
not a thermos flask of tea in sight. Tomorrow,
I will buy peaches, plums, grapes and a watermelon.
I will taste some of this fine, home-cured salami.
Mario and Giovanni will lie under the oak trees.
Mario will keep on pointing out the sights:
*This cathedral façade is made of pink and white marble, Giovanni.*
*Here is the beautiful beach of Viareggio. Here is the Eternal City....*
*If it were possible, I would stay in Rome forever.*
*I would go to the opera. Do you like the music of Puccini, Mario?*
*Yes, but my sister prefers the music of Giuseppe Verdi.*

Tomorrow, there would be another train,
another picnic basket. If it were possible,
I would lie under the trees, with Mario, Giovanni;
their long, straight legs, their ink-dark eyes.
I would lean on bridges. *Bello, bello. Bello, bello.*

# Travelling to the Fish Orchards

We all want the stories.
Why that church was built there, why that island
abandoned – the banana plants and palm trees making
half the arc of a path through the botanical garden
past the glass houses.

We want the names too, the facts, the dates:
his cruel silhouette against a red-gold wall, the sleeve
all flowers, his name that sounds like aubergine.
Then the map of the family, the years in a line –
like railway stations with someone always waiting,
hat in hand on the platform,
who will say at the breakfast table later
*That was where we went... then there.*

But there are times when we take off our glasses,
enjoy myopia: lights blur, the bay is a roaring mouth,
the delicate tower a slim golden finger,
gargoyles' lips are wide brass trumpets,
a flagpole the long, twisted horn of a unicorn
vanishing down an alley.

Or we stumble on words and make strange monsters
out of translation – like the time I grew peaches then fishes
out of the milk-green canals of an island.
The men traipsed their feet
through the thick, damp undergrowth,
waited under trees in abandoned valleys
for the golden scales to shine.

# Mosaic-making

The sky is hard and cracks easily –
bits of blue that let in grey light,

and a bird with one wing hangs
upside down, sings a stone pause.

The landscape makes splinters, every path
leads to a gap. You balance on edges,

you wait and listen, looking both ways
before you cross the line, walk

into the dark. Tomorrow comes sun
like a broken egg. All the yellow squares

have been cracked in the bowl.
They will ache into place,

remembering how it was once
to fit together.

# The Square of the Abandoned Clothes

Following the elephants, the festivals,
we came upon all those clothes laid on paving stones
in the middle of that vast windy square of an Indian city.

Rainbow clothes: skirts, scarves, pantaloons,
thin buttoned blouses, lonely black stockings,
saris stretched out in sheets of gold-stitched purple,
tiny slips of underwear rolled into gutters like so many leaves,
a little girl's dress – something a doll had forgotten,
a shiny pair of lime-green running shorts.

Clothes filling the square, staring flatly up at the sky.
And no-one there. As if all their owners
had laid them carefully down, walked off naked
to another city, found a different way of being, new words
for drapery and buttons, new words for not needing them at all.

Or as if they had thought they might return in the night,
next week, next year, and see themselves lying there,
waiting, under the moon, and decide again
that was who they were; gather the material, strange and warm,
up in their arms, smell the bodies that once were inside,
and breathe new life into them.

# The Dye-Maker

*Dye recipes were jealously guarded secrets. Sometimes they were even bequeathed to the objects of unrequited love in the dye-maker's will.*

Oriental Rugs: Antique & Modern

Take cinnabar, indigo and alum –
you will have to climb hills, pull roots from rock
so you have the smell of it under your fingernails
and it will come back to you when you want it
least: turning a page, drawing a hand through
your hair.  All the rooms full of it.
Grind and sift lighter than dust –  these are the long hours
that will crack your fingers, coarsen your palms.
They will be hard for you who counted effort
as untruth, who having lost an instinct could never
have it back.  There were even jokes you could never
laugh at a second time because the moment had gone.
Soak for ten hours, then drop the wool in and leave
to stain – this will be that feeling that invades you
so you cannot lift your head. The rooms will all be
one shape, one long, distant shade of purple.
And sometimes the days will be indecipherable too.
Mondays, Thursdays... you will not see them pass.
December will follow December.
Boil for three hours and wash in fresh water – still
there will be silence and the windows all steamed up.
You will write your name backwards on the glass,
but you will never see it right. You will stare and stare
at that vat of blue, the only blue you wanted.
Wash the wool again and beat in water – nothing
can rid you now of that spreading stain, its slow invasion.
Stare into the pool now you know its secret.
Observe how your fingertips have turned to blue.
One day every pore will breathe it.

# Dogs at the Harbour

Scruffy brown dogs with oversized heads
and mongrel attitude. They come down from the village
– a bar, sixteen houses and hillside silence –
to bark at a boat.

They do it every hour, frisk ankles and shoes
with tails and noses, attack grocery bags
with a scuffle of paws.

When the last visitor is landed, last bicycle pedalled off
through the scrappy pines down past the canal,
they bark once more at the open sea, at the blink
of the lighthouse, at the nothing that comes back –

just to hear that sharp brown echo return, its slap on water
saying *Nobody comes for you. Nobody waits. This long blue line
is just a horizon that recedes and recedes
and never arrives.*

But what surprises is their full-speed return
as their up and down bodies cover the road
back to the village, as their optimistic tails wave past
the hedgerows, lighted windows and doors.

No pause in their hope
till the next time.

# Orkney Grandfather

*Once he started that printing lark,*
*I knew he'd never come back.*
          Letter from my great-grandfather

He dreamed in type: ink on the waves,
pieces of lead encrusted with salt leaving marks
along the sand. He followed seagulls, made gaps

in the sky where he'd slip out of space –
under a stone, inside a shell,
watching afternoons the men in their boats

sailing round and round their seven tides,
treeless, no colour for safety, no cup of warm.
He spoke not a word, and then he spoke

volumes – all red-spined and purple, a film
of gold dust on the edge of his finger tips.
And he spoke to the sea for he knew it

would never answer, would fling his words
back to him, the slap of bladderwrack,
the scrape of stones: again, again, we cannot

hear you; again, again, you have not made us
understand. Not your cup of fear, not your mad
midnight aqua vita, not your poor stripped board

with its silence of cheese. Not your waiting chair
that itches with impatience: a patina of trouser,
a dark doe eye, another rising sun, another heavy

moon. Not your leaving – not returning;
all those shiny wet words that slowly ran dry
in the gap between here and there.

# The Rider and the Rocking Horse

I gather sleep in the country:
it is the colour of bleached gold,
can be caught in the rim of a saucer.

I drop pennies for thoughts
in a dark brown water butt
and never hear a sound;

a face looks back at me, smiling silence.

In the garden, I watch pears ripen slowly
to the colour of warm green glass,
twisting in spirals under the leaves.

With the creak of the years,
the rocking horse tilts to and fro at the window,
but goes nowhere.

For the maps are in the chest
smelling of lavender and dark grained wood,
creased with the sure thumb of contentment

(trace the line along the edge).

Sometimes I need to lift the lid:
to be sure they are still there,
to find the spot marked *You are here*.

# Paintcharts

The names are spells:
duck eggs warm and held in the hand,
a twist of glass found somewhere on a beach
or a cough drop you suck for hours against your tongue
like a hard shiny bead.

They are the taste of memory
scratched out of the dark –
the way that fireworks came.

In the house I paint them for days and days
till all my muscles ache: shoulder, neck,
a wrist that twitches at night against the pillow.

They will not let me sleep:
blue cornfields moving brushstroke on brushstroke,
the sea a weight of red and terracotta
that stains my toes at the edge of the sand.

I feel them with my fingertips
in cracks and holes – the thickness of egg yolk.
I trail their footprints across the stairway.

I know that any moment now
I'll open the door,
step into their light – ceilings balanced

on a long, white breath, purple cat purring
from a blue armchair, the radio droning
blurred orange voices from a distant room.

# Counting the Dots

*After* The Bridge at Courbevoie *by Seurat*

Days in this foreign city
when I forget my name, when I cannot order
even a coffee or a beer – my tongue a-tangle
with too many vowels, when I am invisible
to shop assistants, and the bus
does not stop for me.

Days when I disappear
into nothing, standing on this bank
smelling the brown French clay, the snatch
and gone of autumn. From the bark against my hands
of the one black leafless tree, from the concrete groyne,
from the nudge and drag of boats at the quayside,

I shift into smoke, the issue from a steamer funnel
smudging the horizon, blurring the opposite bank,
the glitter of glasshouses that I know are there,
the clear procession of tomorrow which is Wednesday
towards Thursday, Friday –

a neat flotilla of boats in a line.
I count their invisible masts to make sense come,
count dot on dot on dot. All dots. Till I disappear.
Till I begin to count again.

# Charting the Progress

Now the clothes fall away with alacrity,
and we avoid the hitches of buckles and belts,
the jeans that bunch as you get to the ankles, the socks
that you forget – with comic effect.
Learned to leave them in a neat pile by the bed.

Now the hands know geography,
detailed as an A to Z. And we understand
that bodies are road maps or electrical circuits –
a twist of a nipple, a current of fingers through the hair.
As logical as science after all.

Now our kisses are easy and wet
with a probing tongue – not shy and dry as blotting paper.
And we know the dangerous words
to leave out – those yearning verbs – even *sotto voce*.
Stick to simple, unloaded nouns.

Now, after twenty years (your plane delayed,
semi-drunk on your mini-bar's stolen champagne),
we remember the first time, the mumbling, the fumbling,
crash of the rain outside, and some stoned student upstairs
singing *All you need is love*.

# On Re-seeing *Jules et Jim*

In middle age, unreal middle age –
years like snow, the soft and silent stealth
of their covering – I wake without love,

sheets adrift, lines of clear, white light
through the blind. Wake too with a sense
of having learnt content, a here-and-now content,

a ceasing of the raging – oranges balanced
against the blue of the table top, spherical,
poised, knowing their weight. Then, outside,

a tree taps light branches on the window,
fingers on a memory drum, and those moments
burn back untouchable behind glass, make

a gesture of sound, a something untranslatable.
These are the days when an old film forces tears,
absolutes steadfast against passing trains, clouds, a river,

all those black and white faces waiting for colour.

# Runner

*In memoriam JS*

Maths was torture to you, round the class reading
of *Julius Caesar* made you blush bright red,
and your spelling defeated us all.

In the music lesson you listened diligently for the beat
but never ever got it, though I can see you now
through the rehearsal room porthole window –

banging timpani, arms flailing wildly like someone drowning,
tip of your tongue curled round your upper lip,
eyes shut tight, banging and banging,

till someone complained, the way they always did complain
about you. Only your running blew them away,
your trainers' white soles flashing through the woods,
luminous then gone. *Where's he off to?* they'd mutter,

half-certain you were up to no good, then begrudging you
a little praise, then amazed at the speed of you

as you ran away, leaving the whole school behind you,
ran through tramlines of white paint on grass,
ran through summer – made air stand still,
ran into the sun (we put our hands across our eyes
                                             to watch you).

You took us with you to as far as we could go.
We saw you break the thin, white tape, still not believing.

# Army Sewing Kit

I had never seen him sew in my life.
Not a button. Not a hem.

Now here was this tiny package – and him telling me
how every man had been taught to use it.

Six round buttons in three different sizes,
tough khaki twine, red and white cotton thread
around a cardboard band, four pins
and a single gold-tipped needle.

His large square fingers became suddenly deft,
pulled the twine against the light,
through the needle, through one spinning button,
then down flat against the cloth.

And suddenly he was sewing for his life.
He had no son, no room to clear, no house
to move. There was just this moment.

Then the next. The silence and the terrible noise
inside the silence. Then the button anchored
tight at the edge of the collar. I could see it

right against his Adam's apple, and him
swallowing hard again and then again.

# After the Piper

Once they had gone, we kept on
hearing their voices, checked ourselves
at kerbs and corners to catch hold
of their hands – telling them *Watch the wheels.*

We stacked our supermarket trollies
with their favourite foods: sugar puffs,
spaghetti rings, Mr Men yogurts,
and called them down to empty chairs at tea tables.

Later, we washed up a clean, shiny plate
and a knife and fork – almost for something
to do. Anything other than cry for them,
that seemed like not believing.

But only the rats came back. This time
we let them go about their business,
heard them at night pattering behind
the skirting board while we slept upstairs,

felt their blind, pink babies sniffing curious
at our fingers, watched them sliding
like scared skaters across the parquet floor,
and thought of them almost tenderly.

# Full Moon

*After Lorca*

No-one eats oranges beneath a full moon.
The taste of too much fullness hurts,

leaves a hunger, a space,
a stain on empty fingers.

Better eat green and icy fruit instead –
enough for the tongue to taste

and live on, curling round the rim
of your teeth, lingering from Monday

to a maybe moonless Tuesday.
Till back it sails full and orange

into your next expectation's sky.

# The Tightrope Walker's Retirement

This strange solidity of red French soil
under my feet. Flinty cubes of gravel
lodged in the toes of my sandals.

A recurring disbelief
that this garden path leads somewhere
else as concrete as here.

Another veranda. Another house.
A wall for the suckers of ivy
to cling to.

Such unbelievable tenacity
of one material thing to another.

At my back this hoop of wicker –
ribbed like bone, holding in flesh.
This ageing flesh.

In front of me the light:
this lovely unknowability of air
and the changing alphabets

of cigarette smoke –
ring on ring; only sound
the motion of birds' wings.

I feel their remembered rush
of blood and air, the wonder
of not falling;

study inch by inch
the kitchen maid's washing line
pearly with morning rain.

# The Book of Milan

*Certo il cuore ha sempre qualche cosa da dire*
*su quello che sarà, ma che sa il cuore?*
*Appena un poco di quello che è gia accaduto.*

*Certainly the heart has something to say*
*about what will be, but what does the heart know?*
*Only a little bit of what is already past.*

Alessandro Manzoni, *I Promessi Sposi*
*(The Beloved)*

# Milan Diary

They write to me as if I winter abroad:
geraniums on the window sill, wide open sunlight,
snow like sleep on top of the mountains.

But there is strange fog over the city. Rain.
I stand on the balcony, hold fast to its railing, peer into
the shape of nothing.

Even in December, sleepy mosquitoes bite
my white English skin. The unfriendly touch
of winter marble. Trains at night rattle my windows.

Every day, I learn a new word, but there is
still more of strangeness. I roll it round on my tongue,
and lose its shape. I make love sound so hollow –

those words being spoken somewhere else
like a television switched on in a room across the road.
The taste it leaves on my lips.

I lick them dry in the dust of the underground,
watch the people together in patterns that fit. But my elbows
are awkward. My hands don't know the gestures,

and my English feet are far too wide –
so I walk into puddles. Even when I laugh,
I know I laugh too loud.

# Shutters

Not the kind I like. Not that half-smile, that one hand
always half-way through the hair – eyes looking

between fingers, cigarette smoke; that shifting move
from foot to foot. Preferred the friend even –

easier, eye to eye, laughter looping across the room.
Not even later in the half-light, exchanging words

like unfamiliar coins, a spill of milled edges against
the formica. We were two shadows waiting

on the white wall, glint of wine, and the round
and round voice of Billie Holliday – till the needle stuck

and the slats of shutters made lines across your face.
I watched a mouth opening, words in the smoke;

watched eyes, an eyebrow lifting out of sight,
the bars of blackness in between. Not this one.

# Translations

I have taught you the time
in English. You have taught me
the words for 'fuck' and 'suck'
in Italian. In between,
we inhabit a surreal world
where my English house is not built
of bricks but madmen,
where you praise the sky-bright
blueness of my ears.

# Tilt

Coming away from your lips,
I hold you there, watching.
I tilt the taste till

I am almost at the edge,
dangling dangerous.
Somewhere down below

I left the sky – electric purple,
the upside-down cathedral,
lighted windows in the bottom

of a canal. Next time
I breathe, I know I'll land
on red roof slant, tiles –

my hands holding fast
to the spinning bird
of a weather-vane.

# At *La Scala*

Now we are at the opera,
listening to love in the purest vowels

as the fat lady sings 'my heart like a bird,
like the bud of a flower',

as the soldier puffs his chest out wide,
waits for the fatal bullet,

as the fat lady (again) waves a fat white hand
and leaps to die from a swaying battlement.

Ridiculous, I know, but this is what
I am good at: beginnings and endings.

In between, we shuffle our programmes,
anticipate the flavours of the ice-cream seller:

traditional vanilla, strawberry whirl,
death by chocolate.

# English Lesson

We are doing Chapter 6: Hobbies, *I like doing…*

Roberto is playful and wants to talk about sex in cars
and gear sticks. We lose ourselves in body parts:
engine, carburettor, *vroom, vroom.*

Carla likes cooking, the *gnocchi*
her grandmother taught her how to make –
a whole day set aside, potatoes in piles,
all the family peeling. We all mime with her.

Giancarlo bicycles twenty kilometres every Sunday
(we imagine his overfed thighs in Lycra and laugh).
He lists all the cups he won; his podgy hands making circles,
his moustached mouth the whirring of spokes.

Gianni goes back to his village, kisses his seven little sisters,
counts his rows of tomatoes, his *zucchini*, his big *zucchini.*
He wears different shoes, screwing his face up
at buckled black leather. No briefcase. No boss.

Francesca likes going to the mountains, the lakes, the sea –
wherever her friends have houses. We are all invited.
When you open the windows all the houses have
                                   beautiful views,
and there is *panetone* for breakfast. Like Christmas.

Franco likes playing cards in the bar with his friends.
Same bar, same friends. Every evening playing poker
at Vittorio's place. He counts the years on his fingers
as if he has never counted before.

Lucia says she cries all weekend, every weekend –
since Massimo left her. She sits in the flat and cries.
There is nothing else to do.

The silence pulls at her words, dangling cut-out and foreign
on the air, begging to be mistakeable: a disappearing trick
against the classroom's white walls.

Then Roberto claps his hands. He meant to say
he likes practising his English. We all groan.

# Fog

Creased and blood-warm, the bedroom hung
suspended in it, shutters flung back
to greyness against the glass. You already

somewhere else – grinding coffee beans,
shaving or washing off intimacy,
bathroom steam snaking through the apartment.

Or waiting early mornings on the station platform
while you drove to work at the hospital,
hearing the slow arriving of the all-

stopping train to Milan but never seeing it
like sleep-walking into absence. Or standing
three feet from the cathedral façade, unable

to make out anything, just a blindness
of grey and some imagined perception of devils
and angels – fingers searching out the edge

of a wing, a scaly tail, the stone sound
of a trumpet. Or driving the long way round
past the canals: the tops of the fishermen's rods

all in a row – fine black lines appearing
out of nothingness. I imagined their silent faces
rimed with wet and cold, staring hard at a flash

of fins on the sightless air, water dripping
onto their boots; the fish all stiff and glassy-eyed
by the time the sunlight found them.

# Drowning

Once I made myself almost drown
because of you. I wanted to swim
so far out of my depth and know

what being on that edge would feel like.
Afterwards, sick and retching on the beach,
I began to hallucinate: I was standing

at the end of the Milan motorway
in front of one of those smoking bonfires.
Naked under a white fur coat,

I was a Brazilian transvestite
with inch-long eyelashes, maraschino lips,
trying to tempt you with the curve of my breasts.

# House in the Mountains

Now we are in the mountains –
vast, miniaturised. Your breath
against the glass, the drift of mountains
into clouds. No colour to hold,
just a slow fall into whiteness. You freeze
before you touch my limbs, my hands.
I lie in stone, in sculptured sheets fold
on fold. Snow will cover us: wine glass,
boot, a multi-coloured ski-jacket
thrown across a chair. Our words
have long ago hung chandeliers on the air.
Cut-glass, reflecting vacant light, they drop
with the coolness of stainless steel knives.

# Invisible

I was never there – in all those places
we travelled together.

Ask your best friend Beppe
(who always lies for you), ask your parents
about the postcards they received –

'you were doing a course for the hospital,
you were visiting that favourite aunt
(the one with Alzheimers, who talks to her tomatoes)'.

In all your photographs I am edited out,
remaindered in a drawer, at most a profile
by a curtain.

So you won't find me again that easily,
the never there,

                who came in the morning
all over the sheets, before the hotel maid took them out
for the wash,

                    who lay by your side
in the up and down sound of your breath –
giving just one rhythm to the bedsprings' creak,

who slid inside your mouth, right down
to the bottom of your chest
so we made a single shadow as we slipped away.

# The Bright Dresses

After your *addio* - breathless, banal, the click
of the telephone, I came out into Corso Vittorio Emmanuele.
Milan's glorious main street: rows of posh shoe shops –
buckles and toecaps on tip toe behind thick glass;
at the end of the boulevard the cathedral spires like the tails
of old seahorses: ridged, brittle and upside down;
sunlight all round me in a hot, close envelope with its smell
of coffee and expensive brief cases; words on the air
from the English lesson I had just been teaching:
*'Sylvia never arrives late. Tom loves pop music*
*and small dogs.' This is the present simple for habit. It goes*
*on and on I was saying.* Then down the road they came:
three bright dresses in yellow, pink and peacock blue,
blurring to blobs of floating colour inside the tears
in my eyes. They jangled the words, advanced unbearably bright
towards me: *'Sylvia loves pop music. Tom never arrives late.*
*Small dogs. Small dogs. Never. Loves'*.

# Moustache

All the hair I grew then!
Those sideburns, beards,
handle-bar moustaches –
which made me look
adult, teacher, someone else.
And the first thing I did
to prove my indifference,
my out-of-love with you,
was to bare my upper lip.
I have the photo...
There's my thin white face,
my mouth exposed.
How on earth did I imagine
such loss could ever convince?

# At Central Station, Milan

The great arch of it. A cathedral of glass
where no bells swing. Only the incantation
of name on name, whispered at windows:

Roma, Firenze, Pavia, Bergamo.
I pay you for otherness, for perhaps –
for the feel of earth sliding under my feet,

for the words I fling in handfuls
into your space like a lung. To breathe
the definitions of finish, which makes

a something of uncountable continuation,
second on second of it. Which makes
a something against the rush of leaves,

the fence poles that flicker and fidget
at my eye, the pale hanging face that might be
mine out there on the window, on the night.

# Stations

Not being Catholic, I do not understand
your stations of the Cross, your bunches
of cellophane-wrapped flowers at bus-stops and hairpin bends,
your pyramids of votaries.

But there are places all over this city
which burn with the passage of our presence.
A café thick with Futurist daubs.
Green in the sun, one of those long canals edged by rusty
                                                          balustrades
where the washing hangs in strings and a voice is always
shouting over music.
A picture in the corner of the Brera with your half-smile,
your eyebrow vanishing into the dark,
only held in place by some monstrous gilded frame.
The vast dusty glitter of a ballroom
where gay men dance the cha-cha-cha with a gentle grace,
their hands barely touching
their partners' lower backs.

I honour these our 'stations' on sliding trams,
behind the condensation of a packed bus window.
Or trudging through snow when Milan is traffic-less, grounded
I grind the sand and grit into the white,
find the pavement squares with the edge of my toe
and stare up at some closed café window –
to make the sign of 'I did, I do, I don't know why'.

## Acknowledgements

'First Marriage' and 'The Tightrope Walker's Retirement' were
both commended in the National Poetry Competition (1997 and
1998); 'Water Tank' won first prize in the London Poetry
Competition, 2000; 'Runner' won second prize in the London
Poetry Competition, 2001; 'Army Sewing Kit' was shortlisted for
the Forward Poetry Prize (Best Individual Poem), 2001;
'Paintcharts', 'Icarus Writes Home' won prizes in the Tabla
Poetry Competition (2000); 'The Summer of Doing Things
Differently' and 'Windswept' were both commended for the
Housman Poetry Prize (1998, 2000); 'My Father's Wedding
Gloves' and 'After the Piper' both won first prize in the Ripley
Poetry Competition (1998, 1999); 'The Rider and the Rocking
Horse' won first prize in Harlow Poetry Competition, 1997;
'Wedding' and 'Counting the Dots' were both shortlisted in
London Writers (1997, 1999); 'The Tightrope Walkers' Wedding'
won fourth prize in Lancaster Poetry Competition, 1999; 'The
Goodbye Letter' won third prize in the Yorkshire Poetry
Competition, 2000; 'Pumpkins' won third prize in the New
Forest Poetry Competition, 2000.

Twelve of the poems in this collection appeared in *Anvil New
Poets 3* (2001). 'Counting the Dots', 'The Dye-maker',
'Paperweight' and 'Answerphone' appeared in *Reactions 2*,
published by UEA (2001). 'The Square of the Abandoned
Clothes', 'Runner', 'Windswept' and 'The Goodbye Letter'
appeared in *Reactions 3*, published by UEA (2002).
'The Bright Dresses' was commended in the EFL Poetry
Competition (1999); 'The Bright Dresses' and 'English Lesson'
appeared in *Poetry as a Foreign Language*, published
by White Adder Press.

Poems in this collection have also appeared in *Poetry Wales,
Ambit, Stand, Envoi, Smith's Knoll, Poetry London, Tabla, Blade*
and *Staple*.

With special thanks to the Thursday Group, and especially
Jane Duran, for all their support and inspiration.